# Great Fiddling Tunes

# CELTIC GEMS

**by Craig Duncan**

Online Audio

To access the online audio go to:
*WWW.MELBAY.COM/30860MEB*


*WWW.MELBAY.COM*

# Preface

*Celtic Gems* contains 103 of the most played and loved traditional melodies from the Celtic tradition. There are 40 jigs, 10 slip jigs, 40 reels, 3 strathspeys, 2 Irish-style hornpipes and 8 airs and waltzes included.

Tunes of similar style and tempo are grouped together, with melodies that work well in sets, or medleys, found on the same or adjacent pages. This collection is useful for "sessions" and ceilidhs as well as for adding to your Irish, Scottish, and Celtic repertoire.

Suggested chord changes as well as stylistic bowing and ornament ideas are included to give the musician options interpreting the tunes.

A companion online audio recording of each tune includes the fiddle melody with guitar accompaniment. The recordings are performed at a medium-slow tempo to aid in learning and practicing.

These tried and tested melodies are fun to play. I wish you great joy and success in performing these tunes.

# Index of Tunes

# Atholl Highlanders

Scottish Jig

# Jig of Slurs

Scottish Jig

# Wi' a Hundred Pipers

Scottish Jig

# Out on the Ocean

Traditional Jig

# The Shores of Lough Gowna

Traditional Jig

Note: This tune is also played one step higher in B minor.

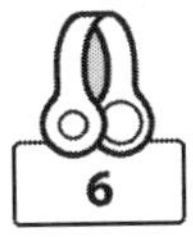


# The Ship in Full Sail

Irish Jig

# The Killavil

Irish Jig

# The Connaughtman's Rambles

Irish Jig

# The Cliffs of Moher

Irish Jig

# Banish Misfortune

10

Irish Jig

# The Lilting Banshee

11

Ballinasloe Fair

Traditional Jig

12

# Drummond Castle

Scottish Jig

13

# Lads of Dunse

Traditional Scottish

14

# The Stool of Repentance

Traditional Scottish

15

# Merrily Kiss the Quaker

Irish Jig

16

# Maggie Brown's Favorite

Irish Jig

17

# Apples in Winter

Irish Jig

18

# The Monaghan Jig

Irish Jig

19

# Trip to Sligo

Irish Jig

20

# Tobin's Favorite

Irish Jig

21

# St. Patrick's Day

Slow option ♩. = 62-72
Jig tempo ♩. = 106-116

Irish Jig

22

# Garry Owen

Irish Jig

23

# The Muckin' o' Geordie's Byre

Scottish Jig

24

# The Hills of Glenorchy

Scottish Jig

25

# Cherish the Ladies

Irish Jig

26

# The Piper's Weird

Adagio

J. Scott Skinner

27

# Glen Jig

Scottish Jig

# The Buck of Cabrach

J. Scott Skinner

29

# The Priest's Leap

Irish Jig

30

# The Priest and His Boots

Irish Jig

31

# The Priest With the Collar

Irish Jig

32

# The Geese in the Bog

Irish Jig

33

# The Walls of Liscarroll

Irish Jig

34

# The Chicago Jig

Traditional Jig

# Paddy Clancy's Jig

35

Traditional Irish

# Roche's Favorite

36

Traditional Jig

37

# Easter Sunday

Irish Jig

38

# Charley the Prayermaster

Irish Jig

39

# The Mist Covered Mountain

Irish Jig

40

# Paddy O'Rafferty

Irish Jig

41

# The Rocky Road to Dublin

Irish Slip Jig

42

# Dublin Streets

Irish Slip Jig

# Fig for a Kiss

43

Irish Slip Jig

# Hardiman the Fiddler

44

Irish Slip Jig

# Drops of Brandy

45

Traditional Scottish

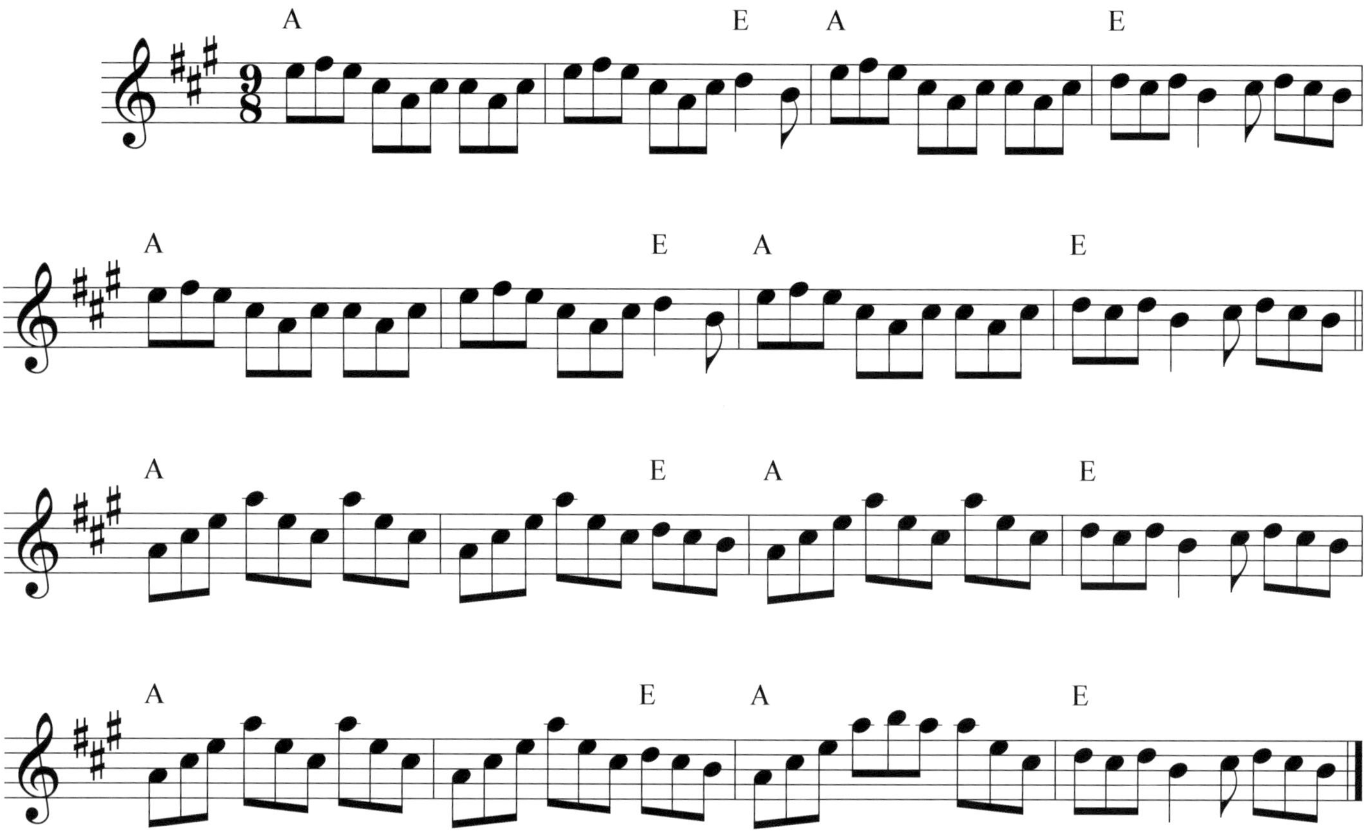


# Brose and Butter

46

Traditional Scottish

47

# I Ha'e a Wife o' My Ain

I Have a Wife of My Own
to be played with Bagpipes

Traditional Scottish

# I Ha'e a Wife o' My Ain

I Have a Wife of My Own
alternate fiddle version

Traditional Scottish

48

# The Butterfly

Irish Slip Jig

49

# Baltiorum

Irish Slip Jig

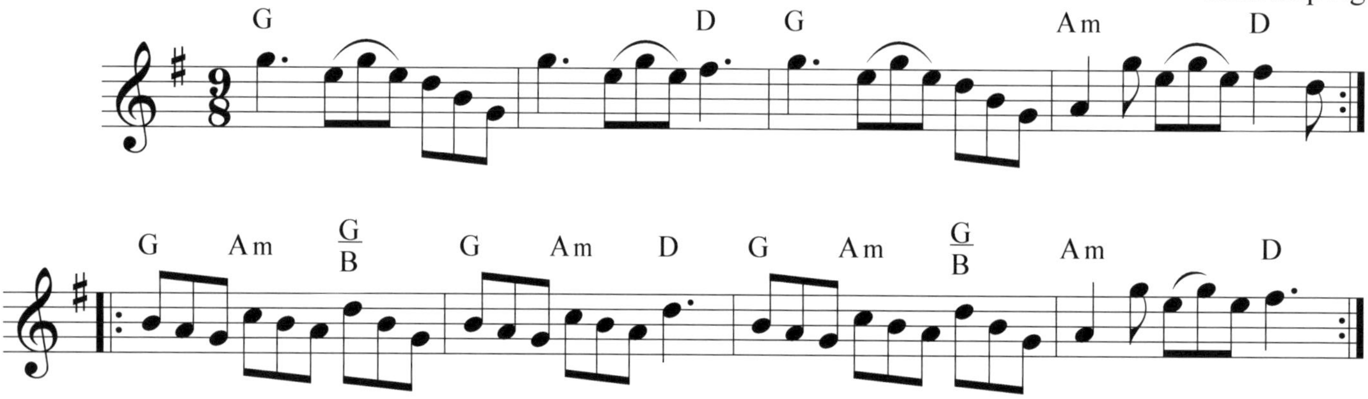


50

# Jack on the Green

Irish Slip Jig

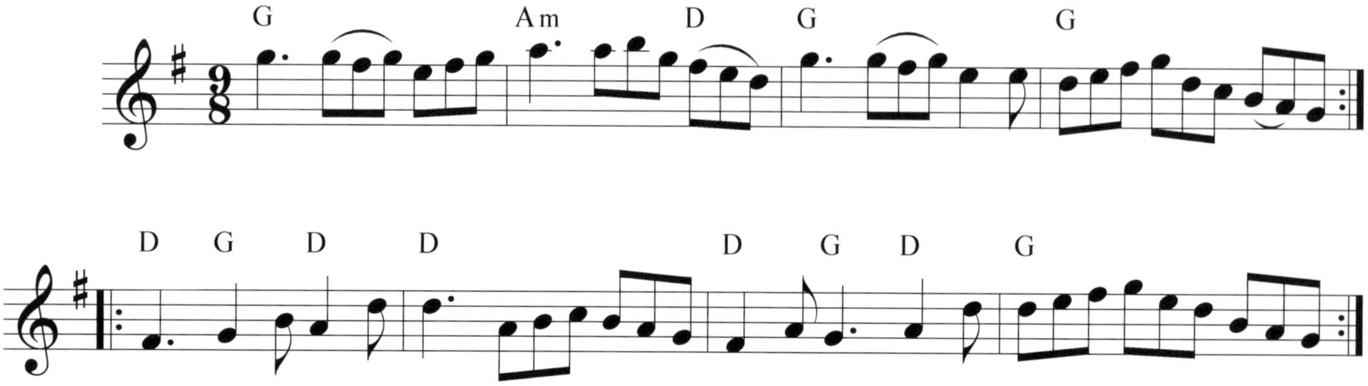

51

# The Source of the Spey

Scottish Strathspey

52

# The Banks of the Spey

Scottish Strathspey

53

# Sweet Molly

Scottish Strathspey

# Sweet Molly

Scottish Reel

54

# Devil's Dream

## The De'il Among the Tailors

Reel

55

# The Star of Munster

Irish Reel

56

# Sporting Paddy

57

# Cooley's Reel

Irish Reel

58

# The Mountain Road

Irish Reel

59

# High Road to Linton

Scottish Reel

60

# Clean Pease Strae

Broun's Reel

Scottish Reel

61

# Mason's Apron

Traditional Jig

Note: This is a two-part tune with a variation on the second part presented in the last two lines.

62

# The Sally Gardens

Traditional Reel

63

# The Humors of Tulla

Traditional Reel

# Wind That Shakes the Barley

Irish Reel

# The Musical Priest

Irish Reel

66

# Salamanca Reel

Irish Reel

67

# The Strawberry Blossom

Irish Reel

68

# Repeal of the Union

Irish Reel

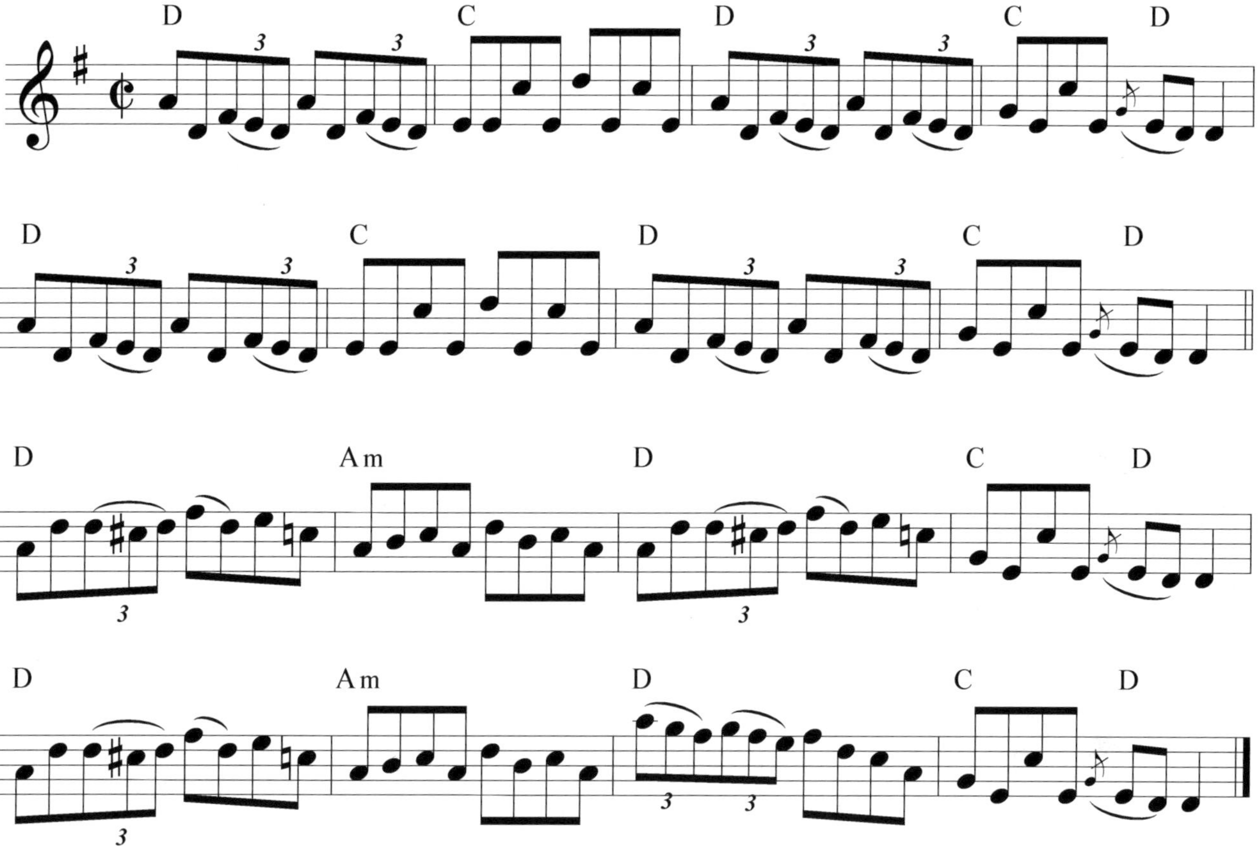


69

# Toss the Feathers

Irish Reel

70

# The Morning Star

Traditional Reel

71

# Miss McLeod's Reel

Traditional Reel

72

# Sligo Maid

Irish Reel

73

# The Green Mountain

Traditional Reel

74

# The Dashing White Sargeant

Scottish Dance

75

# The White Cockade

Traditional

76

# Roxburgh Castle

Traditional Scottish

77

# The Merry Blacksmith

Irish Reel

78

# The Banshee

Irish Reel

79

# Down the Broom

Traditional Irish

80

# Gatehouse Maid

Traditional Irish

81

# Polly Put the Kettle On

Traditional Reel

82

# Molly Put the Kettle On

Traditional Reel

83

# Rolling Down Hill

Irish Reel

84

# The Jolly Seven

Irish Reel

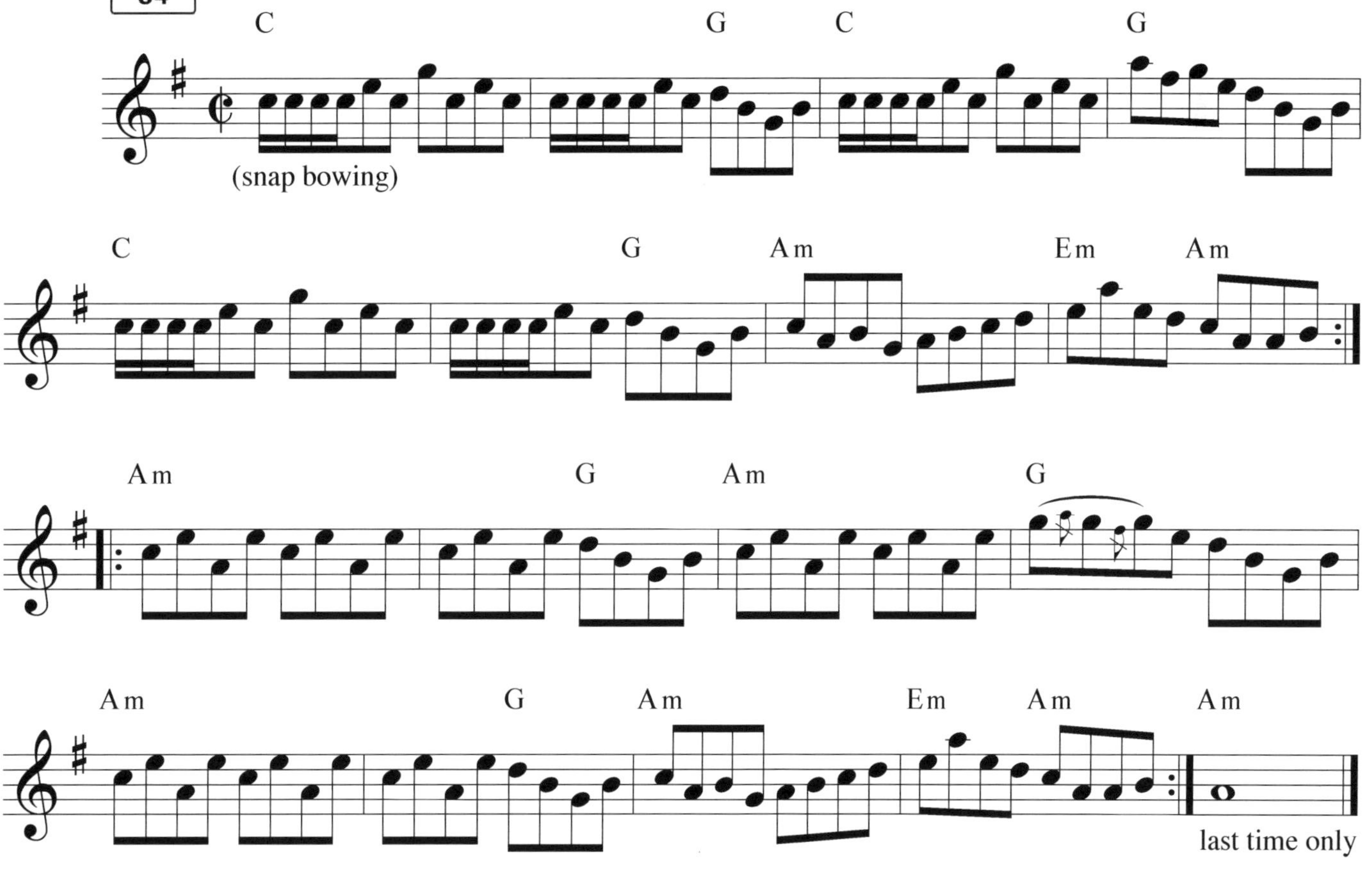

85

# Fairy Dance

Scottish Reel

Note: This fiddle show piece is a two-part tune with variations. It is common for the tune and some variations to be played in the key of G, by moving over one string, or the key of A, by starting on the open A string. The tune usually starts and ends in D.

86

# Loch Leven Castle

Traditional Scottish

87

# Flowers of Edinburgh

Traditional Scottish

88

# Bonny Kate

Traditional Reel

89

# The Bird's Nest

Traditional Reel

# Frost and Snow

Irish Reel

# The Ash Plant

Irish Reel

92

# The Pigeon on the Gate

Irish Reel

93

# Drowsy Maggie

Irish Reel

94

# Off to California

Hornpipe

95

# The Liverpool Hornpipe

Hornpipe

96

# Farewell to Whiskey

Niel Gow Slow Reel

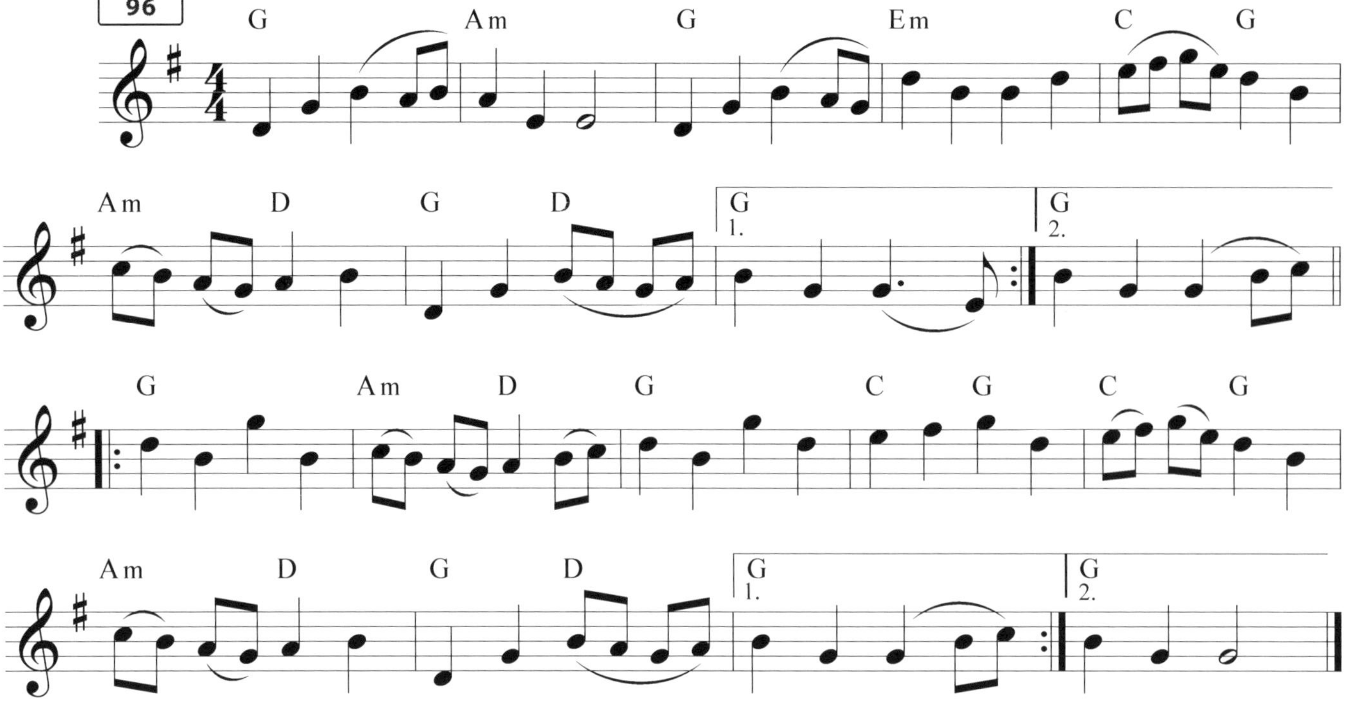


97

# Low Down in the Broom

My Love is Like a Red, Red Rose

Slow Air 1760

98

# The Snows They Melt the Soonest

When the Wind Begins to Sing

Traditional Melody 1821
My Love is Newly Listed

99

# Southwind

An Ghaoth Aneas

Traditional Waltz

100

# Planxty George Brabazon

Turlough O'Carolan

101

# Lord Inchiquin

Turlough O'Carolan

# Planxty Irwin

102

Turlough O'Carolan

# Be Thou My Vision

103

Irish Hymn Tune c. 1000 A.D.